Reach out to Andy Dzurinko, CLU, MEd
about speaking to your group
or to order his books:

INSPIRED: Making a Mark on the World

The Power of Optimism

LOL—Laugh Out Loud: Feel Good and Live Longer

(877) 580-5556
dzurinko@gmail.com

www.thepowerofoptimism.com
www.amazon.com

INSPIRED:
MAKING A MARK ON THE WORLD

INSPIRED:
MAKING A MARK ON THE WORLD

True-Life Vignettes Proving the
Power of Positive People

ANDY DZURINKO, CLU, MEd

Dragon
Press

Tempe, Arizona

INSPIRED: Making a Mark on the World
Copyright 2021 Andy Dzurinko, CLU, MEd

All rights reserved, including the right of reproduction in whole or in part in any form.

Dragon Press
2177 E. Warner Rd. Ste. 102
Tempe, AZ 85284
(877) 580-5556

Website: www.ThePowerofOptimism.com

ISBN Number: 978-0-9721797-4-4 (paperback)

Library of Congress Number: 2021937871

Kingery Printing
P 217-235-7161
800-743-5151
Dragon Press CN48350

Book Shepherd Ann Narcisian Videan, ANVidean.com

Dedication

To Dick and Jane Neuheisel, Harry Mitchell, and Virginia Thompson, founders of the Arizona Tempe Sister Cities Corporation in 1970. Thank you for making the difference in the lives of hundreds of students, teachers, and families in Arizona and countries around the world.

To my brother John Dzurinko; Martial Arts Grand Master Andy Bauman; Sunkist and USA Wrestling Coach James Johnson; and James Harris, M.D., co-author of *LOL—Laugh Out Loud: Feel Good and Live Longer*. These men truly inspired and made a difference in the lives of their families, students, wrestlers, friends, and everyone they touched. They will be missed but not forgotten.
May their memories be eternal.

Acknowledgements

Thank you to the many people who contributed to the publication of this book:

Ande Henninger and Joe Borik: book cover

Leanna McDonald: Photography by Leanna

Mary Fachman, Vince Salotti, Tom Ambrose, Corwin Miller, Dee Dees, Deanna Marquez, Ginger Dzurinko, Carol Vack, and Ann Videan: editing

Jane Neuheisel, Making a World of Difference Vignettes: Tempe, Arizona, Sister Cities

Karl Tribelhorn: Foreword

Anne Montgomery: Epilogue

Professor Keith Brown: Tempe Sister Cities historian

Duane Moore: Tempe Sister Cities song

Vignettes:

William Bennett
Karina Bland
Dr. Anne Borik
Jerry Brock
Patricia Brooks
Dara Dzurinko
Nijmie Dzurinko
Mark Field
Glynn Gilcrease

James Hong
Bradie James
Professor Amal Kabalan
Eric LeGrand
Cindy Lightner
Jaz Limos
Stephen Louis
David Lucier
Dean Mack
Susan Mack
Jim McCloskey
Billy Mills
Richard Obert
Christopher and Dana Reeve Foundation
Paula Pedene
M.G. Peterson
Nishan Rajakaruna
Jim Seybert
John Simpson
Glen Spencer
Dan Sufelt
Andy Talley
Doug Tammaro
Mike Vaccaro
Larry West
Matt Wollersheim
Bob Zambo

Table of Contents

Dedication
Acknowledgements
Foreword   1
Preface   3
Introduction   5

Chapter 1: Giving a Hand Up
A Legacy of Giving:
   John Dzurinko and Nijmie Dzurinko   8
Pay it Forward:
   Author Catherine Hyde   10
A Legacy of Helping Bucknell Athletes—
   Herman "Ham" Bahr   12
Finding Uses for "Waste"—
   John van Hengel, and St. Mary's Food Bank   14
Making a Difference for Children in Foster Care—
   Dan Shufelt   16
Makeovers for the Homeless—
   Jaz Limos and Saints of Steel   18
The Man Behind the Chocolate—
   Milton Hershey   20
Lanny's Legion: Using Sports as a Platform for Education—
   Lanny Van Eman   22
Advocating for Women Writers—
   Patricia L. Brooks   25
Advocate for Veteran Education—
   David Lucier

Chapter 2: Start Something

Building Through Integrity—
 Jerry Colangelo and Phoenix Suns Charities   28
National Veterans Magazine—
 Publisher and Editor Mark Field   31
Founding St. Jude Hospital—
 Danny Thomas   33
Mothers Against Drunk Driving (MADD)—
 Founder Candy Lightner   35

Chapter 3: Inspire Others

Creating a Better World Through Sacrifice—
 Pat Tillman   37
Athletes Do Make a Difference in the Lives
 of Others   39
Education for All—
 Kitambi, Tanzania, Africa   40
Nothing Is Impossible—
 Christopher Reeve   42
"Jersey Strong:" Obstacles as Opportunities—
 Eric LeGrand   44
Supporting Asian Actors—
 James Hong, an actor with 600-plus acting credits
 and counting   46
A Resilient Spirit—By Professor Amal Kabalan, electrical
 and computer engineering, Bucknell University   48
Inspiration from History: Abraham Lincoln's Words
 and Actions—Glynn Gilcrease   50

Chapter 4: Right a Wrong

The Exonerator—
   James McCloskey   53
A Modern-Day Tale of David Vs. Goliath—
   By Paula Pedene   55
A Man, A City, A Cemetery—
   Jerry Brock   57

Chapter 5: Giving Life

Get in the Game—
   Andy Talley Bone Marrow Foundation   60
A Journey of Inspiration in Tackling Cancer—
   Bradie James   62
A Call to Action—
   Kirk Baxter, HIV/AIDS Pioneer   64
The Power of Compassion—
   Maurice Stokes/Jack Twyman   66
COVID-19 Drives Aid to Arizona Indian Reservations—
Stephen Louis   68
Difference Makers in World War II—
   Navajo Code Talkers   70
Aiding Puerto Rico/Latin American Countries—
   Roberto Clemente, #21 Pittsburgh Pirates   73

Chapter 6: 30 Sister Cities Honorees

John Enright—Kafakumba Training Center   75
Dr. James Jackson—Project C.U.R.E.   75
Mona Purdy—Share Your Soles   76
Frank Shankwitz—Make a Wish Foundation   76
C. Mead Welles—A Leg to Stand On   77
Sister Marilyn Lacey   77
Charlotte Gould   78

Hans Vielberth—Hans Vielberth Foundation	78
Irma Turtle—Turtlewill Foundation	79
Austin Gutwein—Hoops of Hope	79
Cindy McCain—HALO Trust, Operation Smile	79
Barbara and Don Liem—Friends of the Orphans	80
Christa Brelsford—Christa's Angels	80
Guy Davidson—Grace Community Church/ International Missions	81
Lisa Hopper—World Care	82
Terry and Anne Guerrant—The Guerrant Foundation	83
Derreck Kayongo—Global Soap Project	83
Edgar Rodas—Cinterandes Mobile Medicine in Ecuador	84
Dr. Raul Osorio—The Osorio Foundation	84
Dr. Brian and Keri deGuzman—4Mati Foundation	85
Dr. John Gillan	85
Maria Keller—Read Indeed	86
Raveen Arora	86
Mallory Brown—World Clothes Line, and Travel Mal	86
Dennis Gerlach—Flying Samaritans	87
Ines and Tracey Allen—IMAHelps	87
Mark Huerta	88
Kenton Lee	88
Kathi Juntunen	89
Michael and Michelle Tessendorf—Orchard: Africa	89
Epilogue—By Anne Montgomery	90

Inspiration

"You Gotta Believe," a vignette from Andy's book The Power of Optimism	93

"The Laughter Cure," a vignette from Andy's book
   LOL—Laugh Out Loud: Feel Good and Live Longer   95
Make a World of Difference/Sister Cities—
   Words and music by Duane Moore   97
List of Tempe, Arizona, Sister Cities   99
Conclusion   100
Request for Review
About the Author

FOREWORD

I have known Andy Dzurinko for more than thirty-nine years. We met in Arizona even though we grew up in western Pennsylvania steel towns in the 1960s only twenty miles apart. His hometown of Monessen, Pennsylvania, helped forge his powerful optimism and desire to make a difference.

Throughout his career as a college athlete, coach, military officer, foundation director, insurance executive, motivational speaker, and author, he has filled ten bucket lists by making a positive impact in the lives of countless individuals.

To quote the famous Scottish Knight, Sir William Wallace, "Every man dies, but not every man really lives." A short quote, but very much applicable to Andy's lifelong philosophy: *Live your life to the fullest, chase your dreams, and make a difference in the lives of others.*

The author of *The Power Of Optimism* has hit another home run with *INSPIRED: Making a Mark on the World.*

—Karl Tribelhorn, West Mifflin, Pennsylvania

Andy Dzurinko

Preface

Making a World of Difference...
How it All Began

By Professor Keith Brown, Arizona State University, historian for Tempe Sister Cities

In 2007, Sister Goretti Ward, a citizen of Tempe's sister city Carlow, Ireland, and now a nun serving in the tiny village of Nuu, Kenya, wrote to Carlow Optometrist Bernard Jennings. She asked him to send her new glasses, as hers were broken.

What did Bernard Jennings do? He went there—to Nuu—at his own expense. Together with two friends, he set up a makeshift clinic and tested everyone in the village... more than three thousand people. Since the locals spoke only Swahili and could not read a traditional eye chart, Barnard made a new chart using pictures of animals in decreasing sizes: zebra, butterflies, etc. His first six patients were totally blind. He found forty-five had cataracts, 215 needed glasses, and some only needed thorns pulled from their eyes.

Bernard arranged for cataract surgeries in nearby Nairobi. He secured glasses for those in need. In addition, he and his team donated the funds they had raised in Carlow to twenty-six orphan girls, making it possible for them to attend school for one year.

Andy Dzurinko

This was a story that needed to be told... and Making a World of Difference was created. Through the years, at least thirty-five world humanitarians have been honored, including Bernard Jennings, English historian and adult educationalist.

My experiences over the years have taught me anything is possible if you want it to be. As you read this book, please keep this in mind. I know it will give you food for thought.

 —Andy Dzurinko, CLU, Tempe, Arizona, 2021

Introduction

I believe making a difference and affecting change starts with you. Hopefully this book will inspire and help you to realize the difference you can make—no matter how big or small.

Over the years, I have considered myself very fortunate when encouraged to help others by people and organizations that make a difference in the world. I find service to others very fulfilling.

Since moving to Arizona in 1989, I became a member of the Tempe, Arizona, Sister Cities program—an organization founded to provide an international exchange program for high school students. These programs change lives. Students learn new cultures, become more independent, find career direction, and see the world in a whole new light. Many want to find ways to make the world better and kinder.

The inspiration for writing this book evolved from my membership with Tempe Sister Cities, and from my belief that one person can help others and make a difference. The idea of making a change globally appears overwhelming, so the TSC created the Make a World of Difference Event. It honors individuals who truly brought aid, comfort, and hope to those less fortunate, whose achievements inspire us, and whose ongoing efforts have reached people around our globe.

There are many different definitions of inspiration and many different ways people are inspired to take action to help others. One definition I like is "a sudden intuition or idea, or something that arouses your desire to take action."

Andy Dzurinko

The question is, what will it take for *you* to gain enough excitement about something that could make a difference in your life and the lives of others in your community?

Do you have the passion, commitment, and motivation to make it happen?

Chapter 1: Giving a Hand Up

"Every morning you are handed twenty-four golden hours… What will you do with your priceless treasure? Remember, you must use it, as it is given only once. Once wasted, you cannot get it back."

—Billy Mills, 1964 Olympic Gold Medal winner

A Legacy of Giving

JOHN DZURINKO AND NIJMIE DZURINKO

By Andy Dzurinko

It all started with my brother John Dzurinko and his influence on our niece Nijmie Dzurinko upon her graduation from the University of Pennsylvania. She expressed her gratitude because, without him, she said she would not have survived.

She explained how he taught her that all human beings want and need the same basic things: to be loved, to be heard, and to be seen. John's legacy was one of loving, giving, caring, and helping anyone at any time. He was not an organizer, but taught Nijmie the skills to communicate effectively with others. As a result of his influence on her she gained a passion for working with youth.

Nijmie is a past executive director of the Philadelphia Student Union (PSU), an organization that gives young people a voice in their education. She began working with them in 1999 and left in 2003 to continue her education. PSU has since trained thousands of young people in its leadership development program.

In 2006, the PSU board invited Nijmie back when the organization was on the verge of shutting down. She built the group back up from a "0" budget and no staff over the next five years. She raised 1.5 million dollars and increased the staff to eight.

To this day, Nijmie is still orchestrating effective change with youth and their ability to influence educational change all over the United States. She is also working with "Put People First." Its mission is to give a voice to everyday people struggling to meet basic needs. The needs to live healthy and fulfilling lives—things like education, housing, healthcare, jobs at living wages, food, and a healthy environment. They work county by county across Pennsylvania, in urban and rural areas, and are politically independent.

John would be proud of you, Nijmie, and so am I.

 Helping others... keeping it in the family!

Pay it Forward

AUTHOR CATHERINE HYDE

The philosophy of *Pay It Forward*, a novel written by Catherine Hyde, embraces the ideas that through acts of kindness among strangers we all foster a more caring society. In the book, a social studies teacher in Atascadero, California, named Reuben St. Clair challenges his students to "change the world." That's something we would all like to do, right? What if we could change the world, even in some small way?

One of the students in the class is Trevor McKinney, who takes the challenge to heart. As he goes about his day, he wonders what he could do, as a twelve-year-old student, to change the world. He starts by showing kindness to a stranger and, from there, moves on to the next person he can help.

Jim Seybert in his book *The One Year Mini For Leaders* talks about how Trevor's kindness is multiplied exponentially across the country as millions of people go out of their way to encourage each other in the way Paul urged the Thessalonians church to do.

The book becomes a movie and the country falls in love with Trevor because what he did was unusual. What can you do to make a difference in your life and the lives of others?
Pay it forward! Give it a try! I know you can do it!

The Pay It Forward Foundation is a 501(c)(3) nonprofit organization, established in September of 2000, by Catherin Ryan Hyde, author of the 1999 novel, *Pay it Forward*. The next year brought the success of the motion picture *Pay It*

Forward, which starred Helen Hunt, the adorable Haley Joel Osment, and even Jon Bon Jovi.

 You, too, can pay it forward!

Jim Seybert, August 7 message
One Year Mini for Leaders
Tyndale House Publishing, Inc.

A Legacy of Helping Bucknell Athletes

HERMAN "HAM" BAHR

By Andy Dzurinko

You've probably never heard of Herman "Ham" Bahr. However, to Bucknell football players like me from the Pittsburgh, Pennsylvania, area from 1958 to 1965, he was responsible for scouting high school student athletes and encouraging us to attend Bucknell University in Lewisburg, Pennsylvania.

"Ham" as he was affectionately known, grew up in the Oakland District of Pittsburgh. He never graduated from high school but took correspondence courses while working as a laborer for the City of Pittsburgh Parks Department. Eventually over the years, he became superintendent of parks for the city.

In January of 2020, I met with a good friend, Tom Ambrose, who had recently lost his wife Alice of fifty-one years. He told me how fortunate he was to attend Notre Dame and to meet Alice who was attending St. Mary's.

His story reminded me of how fortunate I was to attend Bucknell, and to meet the man responsible for that opportunity, Herman "Ham" Bahr.

At the time "Ham" would travel around the Pittsburgh area scouting potential student athletes for Bucknell where Bill Wrabley—his nephew and assistant football coach and a Bucknell graduate—worked with Head Coach Bob Odell.

This was my good fortune. "Ham" recruited many of us and we went on to have success athletically and, more importantly, earn degrees.

My success at Bucknell continued because of the staff and coaches like Bill Wrabley and Bob Odell, and administration and staff like Fitz Walling, Dick Skeleton, Pete Pedrick. These Bucknellians remained at the university and were difference makers not only to me but to all the students.

In addition, people like Sid Jamieson, the long-time lacrosse coach; Brad Tufts, sports information director, and professors like Charles Hollister, Ralph Reese, Phil Harriman, Tom Wilson, and Bob Ewing whose commitment to helping others and caring for students made a difference.

 Bucknellians, thank you!

Andy Dzurinko

Finding Uses for "Waste"

JOHN VAN HENGEL AND ST. MARY'S FOOD BANK

By Susan Mack

A hungry young mother. A man with a mission. And a new goal.

These were the beginnings of the world's first food bank. Back in 1967 in Phoenix, Arizona, John van Hengel volunteered at a local soup kitchen serving dinner to those in need. John struck up a conversation with a young mother and her ten children who frequented the soup kitchen. Curious about her situation, he asked how she was feeding her ten children outside this daily meal. She told him her husband was in prison and, to make ends meet, she was going through dumpsters behind grocery stores.

"You'd be surprised at what those grocery stores throw out," she said.

Van Hengel's heart broke when he heard this, so he came up with the idea of a "Food Bank," where individuals and companies with excess food could "deposit" it and those in need could "withdraw" it.

He took the idea to his local parish, St. Mary's Basilica in downtown Phoenix. They loved the idea and loaned him $3,000, a pick-up truck, and the use of an abandoned building where he was able to turn his dream into reality. In gratitude, he named his food bank "St. Mary's." John and his volunteer friends got right to work approaching grocery store managers. Soon the team was driving around Phoenix daily picking up nutritious food and bringing it back to the food bank.

The first year of St. Mary's Food Bank saw the distribution of enough food for 250,000 meals to struggling and hungry Arizonans. Fast-forward to today, St. Mary's distributes that amount of food five days a week!

He went on to become the founder of several other food banks across the country. Realizing the need for a network of food banks across the United States, John founded the national organization America's Second Harvest, now known as Feeding America.

Years later, John van Hengel founded the Global Food Banking network. He is rightly referred to as "the father of food banking" with it starting right here at St. Mary's Food Bank in Phoenix, Arizona.

Today, St. Mary's Food Bank is one of the largest food banks in the United States, and proud of the impact it has had on Arizona—and the world.

 Food for those who need it most!

Susan Mack, CFRE Director of Major Gifts
602-242-3663
swmack@firstfoodbank.org

Making a Difference for Children in Foster Care

By Dan Shufelt

Early in Dan Shufelt's professional career, he worked at a CPA firm. Its managing partner, Len Miller, told his team to find a charitable cause where they could devote their time and energy. He charged the group with finding a passion and giving back to the community. Len preached the importance of giving one's all to the charitable activity and joining a charitable board to make a difference in the community.

Dan's volunteer path led first to working with the Boys and Girls Clubs, and moved on to join the board of a small nonprofit, Arizona Helping Hands.

Dan progressed from board member of this fledgling group of volunteers, to steering Arizona Helping Hands on a path supporting children in foster care. When it became apparent the breadth of services required an executive to lead them forward, Dan put up his hand and volunteered to help chart the course. Little did he know where it would lead.

As of 2020, Arizona's foster care system oversees more than 14,000 children. Today Arizona Helping Hands is recognized as the largest provider of basic needs to these boys and girls. Victims of abuse and neglect need helping hands to show them there is hope, and every program has that objective.

Giving a child a safe place to sleep, their own twin bed or crib, is the first step. From there, add in clothing, diapers, personal care packages, back to school supplies, holiday gifts, and even a personalized birthday package. All of this is done to spread the message that every child is worthy and loved, and our community cares. Arizona Helping Hands has supplied a bed or crib to more than 17,000 children since 2013. Children who enter the front door of Arizona Helping Hands are greeted with smiles and hugs. From the beautiful kid-friendly lobby, to the bag of goldfish offered to new friends, Arizona Helping Hands shares love with every little visitor.

Everyone can do something to help boys and girls in foster care and bring hope to the most fragile children. The important lesson from Len Miller is being listened to every day at the agency's 18,000 square-foot facility in North Phoenix: —get involved and do something to help.

Dan found his passion, now working as a full-time CEO of Arizona Helping Hands. Every day, he assists families and children in need.

His message: "Go find a cause you can give back to and support, to make our community stronger. Figure out how you will make a difference!"

 All children need our help!

Andy Dzurinko

Makeovers for the Homeless

JAZ LIMOS AND SAINTS OF STEEL

Jaz Limos took a lunch break from her job at Apple in San Francisco in 2016. She walked into a Subway Shop and noticed a homeless man sitting on the sidewalk asking for money. She did not give him any but, instead, bought a footlong sub and gave him half.

When he looked up to accept it, she sensed she knew him. His face had aged, and he was not sober, but his voice sounded familiar. She introduced herself and he sat up, dusted himself off, and told her his name was Edgar and he had a daughter about her age. He turned out to be her biological father whom she had not seen for years.

In that moment, seeing him homeless, she knew she wanted to help not only Edgar but all homeless people.

While working at Apple, Jaz went to barbery school at night and immersed herself in the art of hair care. Inspired by her love of barbery and her passion for volunteerism, the San Francisco native founded Saints of Steel, providing free haircuts and care packages to homeless and underprivileged youth in community centers, shelters, and on the street.

INSPIRED: Making a Mark on the World

She and her nonprofit, with the help of many volunteers, not only serve San Francisco but the United States, providing the homeless with makeovers that lead to employment, housing, and new beginnings.

**Helping the homeless!**

Jaz Limos
Founder and CEO of Saints of Steel
Saintsofsteel.org

Andy Dzurinko

The Man Behind the Chocolate

MILTON HERSHEY

Milton Hershey was born in 1857 in Pennsylvania, more than 150 years ago. As a child, he changed school six times. He missed a lot of school days because his family was moving from place to place. His mom took him out of school after fourth grade so he could learn a trade, which is a kind of skilled job requiring manual skills and special training.

When Milton turned nineteen, he decided to start his own candy business. He had an aunt and uncle who loaned him money to get started. Milton worked very hard for six years, but his business didn't make any profit. He closed the shop and tried opening a new shop in New York. But that store didn't make enough money to cover his expenses either.

Milton did not give up. He continued working with other candy makers to learn more and more. He learned how to make caramel with fresh milk. Then he moved back to Pennsylvania and started a caramel company.

Finally he earned success. In a few years, his business was doing well. He learned how to make chocolate along with his caramel. That's when he created The Hershey Company. He sold his caramel company for one million dollars. That is a lot of money today, but it would buy even more things back in 1900.

Milton understood that most people didn't have as much money as he did, even though they also worked very hard. Milton decided to spend a lot of his money and time helping other people in his community.

He and his wife were not able to have their own children. They gave a lot of their money away to help other people's kids. They built homes to care for orphans. He also built schools. The Milton Hershey School was created to help kids whose families didn't have a lot of money. When Milton and his wife died, they left all their money to the school. It still exists today and more than 2,000 students go there.

Milton Hershey did so many good things for his community the town is now named after him. It's called Hershey, Pennsylvania. He left an important legacy along with delicious chocolate treats for us to enjoy.

 An amazing man!

Milton Hershey Foundation
www.mshersheyfoundation.org

Andy Dzurinko

Lanny's Legion: Using Sports as a Platform for Education

Lanny Van Eman

By Bob Zambo, a native of McKeesport, Pennsylvania, and Lanny's lifelong friend

Lanny Van Eman is a very unique name for a very unique individual. Growing up in McKeesport, Pennsylvania, a blue-collar Pittsburgh suburb, Lanny excelled not only in high school and college basketball but also as a coach in high school, college, and the national basketball association. Participating in sports was a way of life for many young athletes like Lanny who wanted to get an education and walk away from working in the steel mills like their fathers, grandfathers, and uncles.

Hundreds of people have been touched by Lanny over the past six decades. One of his greatest attributes was his ability to see something better in people and helping them obtain a college education. You see, Lanny never forgot where he came from and the people who helped him during his lifetime.

Lanny realized that many of the McKeesport area kids, most from struggling steel mill families, needed someone to show them they could also go on to success. At the young age of twenty, Lanny decided to reach out and help shape their future lives.

 A legacy of helping and giving back!

Advocating for Women Writers

PATRICIA L. BROOKS

Twenty years ago, Patricia L. Brooks lost her youngest sister to lung cancer and began a grief journal that eventually lead to writing her first memoir, Gifts of Sisterhood: Journey from Grief to Gratitude. During this process, she realized the need for a women's writers group in her community in Old Town Scottsdale.

With the support of her husband, she started the Scottsdale Society of Women Writers in 2005 to find camaraderie with other like-minded women wanting to share their stories. SSWW is celebrating fifteen years of success this year. Patricia continues to maintain a membership of seventy-five women writers. With the help of SSWW members, more than half of these women are published in various genres. The others are aspiring to write at all levels to produce books, articles, screenplays, and poetry.

At each monthly meeting, Patricia offers a professional speaker to share expertise on various writing, publishing, and book marketing topics. The women meet for dinner with an opportunity to support each other. Several critique groups have formed as a result of SSWW. They meet outside of the regular meeting.

Patricia has launched two other memoirs, *Three Husbands and a Thousand Boyfriends* and *Sick as My Secrets*, with the assistance of her critique group. In return, she has coached many of the women writing memoirs and reciprocated with feedback and book reviews to dozens who have passed through these meetings.

Andy Dzurinko

Part of the mission of SSWW is to be a format for exchanging ideas and an opportunity to network with other women writers. The goals of SSWW include honoring all genres while valuing women writers seeking to share their stories. These women never stop challenging each other to always write.

A win-win environment for everyone!

www.brooksgoldmannpublishing.com

Advocate for Veteran Education

DAVID LUCIER

David Lucier, a combat veteran who served in Vietnam from 1968 to 1969, had just returned from two overseas assignments: Iraq and Afghanistan. He could see our veterans needed an advocate and decided the first and most important need was to advocate for education. There was literally no infrastructure or system in Arizona to support veterans in their quest for academic achievement at that time. He remembered his parents inspiring him to "step up." So, that's exactly what he did.

David helped pass legislation to make higher education in Arizona more affordable for all veterans, regardless of current residence status. Next he spoke with Arizona State University (ASU) President Dr. Michael Crow about twelve to fifteen elements ASU needed to undertake to help ensure academic success at ASU. From 2012 to 2018, ASU went from fewer than 1,000 veterans enrolled to over 10,000… and the numbers continue to grow.

All of Arizona's institutions of higher education have followed suit. The positive impact on our families, communities, our state, and our nation is immeasurable. This is just one way we say, "Thanks for your service."

David's mom was a Women's Airforce Service Pilot (WASP) and his dad a Lt. Commander in the Navy who served on a destroyer in the South Pacific during WWII.

Andy Dzurinko

"Mom and Dad, thank you for your service, your sacrifice, your love and your inspiration."—David Lucier

 Never too old to learn!

Chapter 2: Start Something

"Those who are happiest are those who do the most for others."

—Booker T. Washington

Andy Dzurinko

Building Through Integrity

JERRY COLANGELO AND PHOENIX SUNS CHARITIES

By Tom Ambrose, Phoenix Suns executive, and author

The summer of 1968 witnessed the first, fledgling months of the National Basketball Association's newest franchise, the Phoenix Suns. The team's small sales staff was more than a little disappointed the local citizenry wasn't showing much enthusiasm for season ticket sales pitches or for the new expansion team. As the grumbling became louder, the team's new general manager, twenty-eight year-old Jerry Colangelo, stepped in to silence the complaining and redirect the negativity into a more positive course of action.

"Look," he said. "This community owes us nothing. It's up to us to go out and earn their respect."

Over the ensuing decades, those words would become the mantra for everything the Suns accomplished, every day, both on the basketball court and in the community. For Colangelo, his staff, coaches, and players, it meant adhering to fundamental values, conducting themselves ethically at all times, and treating others with dignity. He believed they had to be open, fair, and honest in their relationships. Do that, play hard, and the respect will come.

At Colangelo's direction, in the early years of the franchise, the Suns created or supported numerous community programs: a Phoenix Suns/Boys and Girls Clubs basketball league with thousands of kids participating, fundraisers for *The Phoenix Gazette* Youth Fund, the Salvation Army, Special Olympics, the 65 Roses Club of the Cystic Fibrosis Foundation, the Easter Seals Society, and countless other nonprofit groups.

In 1987, Colangelo led a group of investors to purchase the Suns from the team's original owners. The first thing on his priority list was to begin planning a new arena in downtown Phoenix. Not far behind, his second priority was to create a charitable foundation to support youth charities.

Within a year, he assembled a board of directors comprised of community leaders to oversee the formation and operation of the team foundation which became "Phoenix Suns Charities." The concept was to leverage the "celebrity" of the Suns franchise and its players to create major fund-raising events, and direct those funds back to areas of greatest need in the community, especially to those charities focused on maximizing the potential of our youth, and protecting families.

By the time Colangelo stepped away from active management of the organization in 2004, the Suns franchise on the court had amassed the fourth best all-time winning percentage in NBA history. They made the playoffs in twenty-four of those thirty-six seasons, including two trips to the NBA Finals and six appearances in the Western Conference Finals.

Meanwhile, off the court, Phoenix Suns Charities, the foundation created by Colangelo in 1988, has continued its robust support of the community. In just more than thirty years, with the help of an active board of directors and the entire Suns organization, Phoenix Suns Charities has raised and distributed more than twenty-one million dollars for scholarships and grants to local students and hundreds of charitable causes in Arizona. The annual donation figure is now more than one million dollars per year.

Not a bad record for a franchise just trying to earn the respect of the community!

National Veterans Magazine

Publisher and Editor Mark Field

I first met Mark in the 1990s when we both were members of the Arizona Governor's Council on Health, Physical Fitness, and Sports. At that time, he was publishing a tennis magazine in Sun City Arizona, but as an eight-year naval veteran he really wanted to publish a veteran's magazine.

"If you are working on something exciting that you really care about, you don't have to be pushed. The vision pulls you."— Steve Jobs

Mark has always felt there was a place and voice for the national veteran's magazine. Its purpose is to make a profoundly deep emotional impact for every veteran and their communities. Everyone has something positive to contribute to those around them. Find it and use it to help others.

The National Veteran's Magazine is now being read all over the United States. You can find the magazines in VA medical centers, clinics and vet centers all over the country. Look for them in governor's offices, state veteran's directors' offices, state legislatures, along with city, county, state, federal, and tribal government offices. They can also be found at the White House, Pentagon, VA headquarters, FBI, CIA, NSA, and military bases all over the country.

"Any goal will require commitment and sacrifice," Mark said. "I have realized my place in the world with the National Veterans Magazine. I accept the sacrifice that comes with reaching for your life's goals. I am prepared to provide my time, resources, body, and soul to see the National Veterans Magazine become one of the largest, if not the largest, publication in the United States of America, reaching upwards of fifty million readers. I am proud of what we have accomplished so far, and we are still in our infancy! 2021 will be an exciting year for our growth."

Giving veterans a voice!

Mark Field
https://nationalveteransmagazine.com

Founding St. Jude Hospital

DANNY THOMAS

As a young man, Danny Thomas had a simple goal: to entertain people and be successful enough at it to provide for his wife and family. But work wasn't easy to come by.

As he and his family struggled, his despair grew. He wondered if he should give up on his dreams of acting or find a steady job. He turned to St. Jude Thaddeus, the patron saint of hopeless causes. "Show me my way of life," he vowed to the saint one night in a Detroit church, "and I will build you a shrine."

That prayer to St. Jude marked a pivotal moment in his life. Soon after, he began finding work, eventually becoming one of the biggest stars of radio, film, and television in his day.

And as one of the world's biggest celebrities, Danny used his fame to fulfill his vow to St. Jude Thaddeus and to change the lives of thousands of children and families.

Danny's shrine to St. Jude Thaddeus was originally to be a general children's hospital located somewhere in the south. Danny's mentor, Cardinal Samuel Stritch, recommended he look to Memphis, Tennessee, the cardinal's home town.

By 1955, Danny and a group of Memphis businessmen he'd rallied to build the hospital, decided it should be more than a general children's hospital. At the time, the survival rate for childhood cancers was twenty percent, and for those with acute lymphoblastic leukemia (ALL)—the most common form of childhood cancer—only four percent of children lived. They believed St. Jude could help these families with nowhere else to turn. St. Jude would become a unique research institution where the world's best doctors and scientists would work together to cure childhood cancer, sickle cell, and other deadly diseases.

To fund the hospital's annual operations Danny turned to his fellow Americans of Arabic-speaking descent. Danny believed that, by supporting St. Jude, this group of Americans would thank the United States for the gifts of freedom given their parents, and also serve as a noble way of honoring forefathers who'd immigrated to America.

In 1957, one hundred representatives of the Arab-American community met in Chicago to form ALSAC with the sole purpose of raising funds for the support of St. Jude Children's Research Hospital. Since then, it has been responsible for all the hospitals fundraising efforts. Today, as when it opened its doors, families never receive a bill from St. Jude for treatment, travel, housing, or food, because all they should worry about is helping their child live.

 Thank you, Danny and St. Jude's!

Copyright 2019 St. Jude Children's Research Hospital
American Lebanese Syrian Association Charity Inc.
(ALSAC)

Mothers Against Drunk Driving (MADD)

FOUNDER CANDY LIGHTNER

After receiving the phone call every parent dreads when her thirteen-year-old daughter was killed by a repeat DWI offender, Candy Lightner founded Mothers Against Drunk Driving (MADD) in her home on March 7, 1980. Before MADD, there were little to no legal consequences for driving while intoxicated. Her organization transformed American attitudes about drunk driving and successfully fought for stricter laws across the country.

The mission of MADD is to end drunk driving, help fight drugged driving, support the victims of these violent crimes and prevent underage drinking. She was also responsible for helping create legislation to make this act a criminal offence and to determine how tough sentences should be implemented.

Candace received the President's Volunteer Action Award for her humanitarian services to the public and, later, became the president of the We Save Lives Campaign which campaigns against those who drive while drunk, are distracted, or under the influence of drugs.

 Don't drive under the influence!

Andy Dzurinko

Chapter 3: Inspire Others

"I don't want to live in the kind of world where we don't look out for each other. Not just the people that are close to us, but anybody who needs a helping hand. I can't change the way anybody else thinks, or what they choose to do, but I can do my bit."

—Charles de Lint

Creating a Better World Through Sacrifice

PAT TILLMAN

By Assistant Athletic Director Media Relations Doug Tammaro, Arizona State University

Pat Tillman was a professional football player who gave up his pro football career to enlist in the U.S. Army after the terrorist attacks on September 11, 2001. He was killed by friendly fire while serving in Afghanistan on April 22, 2004. The news that Tillman, age twenty-seven, was mistakenly gunned down by his fellow Rangers, rather than enemy forces, was initially covered up by the U.S. military.

April 22, 2004, was one of the darkest days in Sun Devil history with the tragic news Pat Tillman had passed away. It shook the Phoenix Valley—and America—at a level that quite possibly may never be replicated. Our hero was gone.

More than seventeen years after his passing, his legacy not only lives, but thrives and inspires. Since 2008, the Pat Tillman Foundation has provided academic scholarships, professional development opportunities and a national network to empower military service members, veterans, and spouses. These scholars are making a difference in the fields of healthcare, business, public service, STEM, education, and the humanities.

More than 600 Tillman Scholars have received more than eighteen million dollars in education investments at more than one hundred universities across the world.

Andy Dzurinko

Pat's Run takes place every April in Tempe, Arizona. As the second-largest on-campus event at Arizona State University, behind only a football game, more than 35,000 people gather to run, walk, and honor his memory. It has been described as the state's greatest day, and as the day a big city became a small town for two hours.

If the starting point was when someone passed away, followed by the question of who has made the most impact after they are gone, it would be hard to find anyone as motivational as Pat Tillman.

Friendships have been built, educational opportunities realized, and dreams met. Pat Tillman's legacy has made lives better.

Pat once said, "To err on the side of passion is human and right, and the only way I'll live." Those who knew him and others who serve in the foundation live this every day. We will never stop our passion for Pat Tillman.

Out of something bad, something good can happen. Make that something awesome, incredible and wonderful.

**That is what inspired Pat during his lifetime!**

Athletes Do Make a Difference in the Lives of Others

By Andy Dzurinko

I believe it is important to acknowledge and recognize the good and positive activities coaches and players all around the United States and the world contribute to their communities on a daily basis. They are dedicated to men and women athletes, amateur and professional, who help and encourage people of all walks of life to do the right things.

These fine individuals are grateful for the opportunities participating in sports has given them and they want to share their good fortune with others. They truly set an example for all of us who give back, and show how being a role model benefits everyone. They are inspired to do good regardless of race, color, or ethnicity. You, too, can follow their examples and be inspired to help others.

Athletes are "difference makers" on and off the field!

Andy Dzurinko

Education for All

KITAMBI, TANZANIA, AFRICA

By Christopher Wollersheim, Nyamazugo Children's Center board member

Kitambi's journey began in 2003 while selling tourist items on the streets of Arusha, Africa. That's when Dr. Wollenshein visited Arusha with his son, Matt. While touring the city, Matt struck up a conversation with Kitambi who, at the time, expressed an interest in furthering his education. Kitambi needed to take a tour guide course and learn a second language. Matt, with the assistance of a few other individuals, provided the money to help him complete the course. After years of staying in touch, Kitambi contacted Matt with an interest in forming a children's center.

At the center they believe everyone has the right to basic necessities which includes a quality education. Unfortunately, thousands of orphaned children live in Arusha, Tanzania, deprived of homes, supportive families, and educations they deserve. The center provides a quality education to help children pursue respectable careers and follow their dreams.

In October 2012, Andy and his good friend and hiking partner Corwin "The Dude" Miller departed Phoenix, Arizona, for Arusha, Tanzania, Africa. We were on our way to climb Mount Kilimanjaro. While in Arusha, we took a tour of the city and our guide was Kitambi Abdallah Kapungawasi.

During our walks, he shared with us how he discovered his purpose in life to help educate underprivileged children in Tanzania. Kitambi himself came from an underprivileged background and received help from generous people who funded his college education. After graduation, he was inspired to show others in the same position that education is not for a select few but for everyone. This led him to open the Nyamazugo Children Center in Arusha.

The center currently provides shelter, daily care, and education to children. But with your help, they can do much more. They are currently working on a new facility in Arusha that would provide the current one hundred youths with a cleaner, safer, more comfortable home, as well as open other doors to 300 other currently homeless children.

Go to www.nyamazugochildrencenter.org to find out more about Katambi's project to help children in Arusha and to consider making a donation that can make a difference in the lives of the underprivileged children in Arusha.

**Awesome!**

Nyamazugo Children's Center, 2017

Andy Dzurinko

Nothing Is Impossible

CHRISTOPHER REEVE

Christopher Reeve, the actor who played Superman, suffered a devastating spinal cord injury that left him quadriplegic in May of 1995. Thrown from his horse during an equestrian competition in Virginia, he showed everyone the true measure of courage. What he did after the injury is a true testament to who he was and his willingness, along with wife Dana, to do whatever it took to generate interest and support research on paralysis from spinal cord injuries. He became the voice and, more importantly, the beacon of hope for all who live with paralysis.

Thanks to the generosity of many people, the Christopher and Dana Reeve Foundation has made a vast difference in the lives of those living with paralysis. Chris and Dana completely changed the way people think about living with spinal cord injuries.

His courage and approach to life after his injury should be a lesson and inspiration to all of us. It is important to understand that, no matter what happens in life, there can always be something worse. The challenge is to believe in yourself, have faith, and enjoy the loving support of family and friends.

Christopher Reeve never gave up. He stayed positive, maintained a sense of humor and never wavered in his commitment to making a difference for those affected by spinal cord injuries. He lost his battle on October 10, 2001, but his accomplishments will never be forgotten.

 Caring about others until the end!

"Giving up is not an option." *Nothing Is Impossible.* pgs. 23–31, Christopher Reeve
https://www.medicinenet.com/christopher_reeve_and_spinal_cord_injury/views.htm

www.christopherreeve.org

Andy Dzurinko

"Jersey Strong:"
Obstacles as Opportunities

ERIC LEGRAND

By William Bennett, Rutgers University, 1964

In October 2010, Rutgers University football star, Eric LeGrand, sustained a spinal cord injury at his C3 and C4 vertebrae during a fourth quarter play at MetLife Stadium. While the initial prognosis was grim, Eric demonstrated his titan strength by shattering all expectations for his recovery and rehabilitation. However, recovery was not enough.

With close to six million Americans living with some form of paralysis, including 1.3 million spinal cord injuries, Eric harnessed the national spotlight he attracted from his injury to give back to the community and inspire those living with, and impacted by, paralysis. To believe.

Team LeGrand was launched in September 2013 as a fundraising arm for the Christopher and Dana Reeve Foundation to carry forward the legacy of the late Christopher Reeve. Since its inception in 2013, Team LeGrand has raised more than one million dollars for the Reeve Foundation.

Eric not only carries the torch of Team LeGrand's mission, he continuously leads by example. During his time as a participant of the Reeve Foundation's Neuro Recovery Network (NRN), he took part in a rigorous rehabilitation regime, including locomotor training, to re-teach his body how to walk and improve his quality of life. Since beginning therapy, he has regained movement in his shoulders and improvements to his overall health.

From becoming an author, sports analyst for *ESPN*, *Sirius*, the *Big Ten Network*, and Rutgers radio, to a much sought after motivational speaker, Eric has given a voice to the paralysis community to mobilize support for critical initiatives, policies, and cutting-edge research during the past five years.

Since his injury, Eric has shown the world that obstacles can be transformed into opportunities, and he will continue to drive his mission forward until he delivers on Christopher Reeve's dream of a world with empty wheelchairs. To Eric, it is not matter of if he walks again, but rather when.

Obstacles can be overcome!

Andy Dzurinko

Supporting Asian Actors

JAMES HONG, AN ACTOR WITH 600-PLUS ACTING CREDITS AND COUNTING

"Asians were put into a movie or TV mainly as a gimmick," Hong said. "We were never thought of as playing the main roles, the leading people. That's the way it was."

But Hong didn't let Hollywood's narrow lens limit his abilities. He battled stereotypes along the way and it led him to start his very own theater company.

Realizing Hollywood wouldn't be able to provide the roles Asian Americans deserved, Hong set out to carve his own space. Along with actor Mako Iwamatsu, Hong helped organize an Asian American acting group in Los Angeles. Their first production was Rashomon, a stage play based on two short stories written by Japanese author Ryunosuke Akutagawa and adapted into film by Akira Kurosawa.

"That started the industry noticing who we were," Hong said. "We weren't just extras, or gimmick people. We were in a play that we organized. We were the main, lead people. We were the actors. And we commanded attention."

That acting group turned into the legendary theater group, East West Players which was formed in 1965 and still is in operation today. James was one of the original founding members.

"East West Players were formulated to showcase works by Asians, who wrote the plays, who designed the stages, who acted in the plays," Hong said. It was all done by professional Asian people.

At ninety-one years of age, Hong isn't ready to slow down any time soon.

The Asian community thanks you!

Andy Dzurinko

A Resilient Spirit

By Professor Amal Kabalan, electrical and computer engineering, Bucknell University

My belief that I can make a difference in someone's life gives me hope for the future. In the classroom and during office hours, close interaction with my students allows me to discover their true passions. Teaching at Bucknell is a very personal process. It is not just about delivering course material, but it is also about the process of discovering the passion of each student and helping them achieve their dreams.

At the beginning of every semester, I feel like a child in front of a Christmas tree, ready to unwrap new stories. I feel very honored and humbled when students talk to me about their passions, their struggles, what makes them tear up and what inspires them to jump for joy. Whether driven by an urge to do better because their parents worked hard to send them to Bucknell, or an eagerness to find meaning in a new life after escaping a war zone, the stories my students share inspire me.

Helping students navigate their struggles—whether social, academic, or emotional—is what keeps me going. During the fall semester, I helped Emily Bayuk, class of 2021, illustrate optoelectronics concepts for young girls interested in engineering. She has a wonderful talent for writing as well as drawing and illustrating abstract concepts. Emily published her first book, *The Fundamentals of Circuits Made Easy*, and plans to publish more books on the electrical engineering concepts she is learning in her classes.

I am also developing solar backpacks to help students study at night in refugee camps. This summer, funded by Davis Projects for Peace, I accompanied Shehryar Asif, class of

2021, to refugee camps in Lebanon to pilot a solar backpack project. We offered a two-day workshop to an all-girl class. The first day we showed students how to make cars run on solar panels, and the next day we introduced the solar backpack. The experience was one of a kind, but the most inspiring thing about it was to experience firsthand how resilient young people are. The refugee students' living conditions were harsh, but they were the happiest kids I have ever seen. They were eager to learn, playful, and fun.

This spirit of resilience I see in many students—whether in Lebanon or Lewisburg—gives me hope. No matter how gloomy our current situation is—climate change, political division, etc.—I truly believe that the youth have the power and capacity to rise to these challenges. In them lies the secret to the continuity of life. To be a part of that process inspires me daily.

 **Go, Bisons!**

Reprinted from the Winter 2020 edition
of *Bucknell Magazine*

Andy Dzurinko

Inspiration from History: Abraham Lincoln's Words and Actions

GLYNN GILCREASE

Glynn Gilcrease is a trial attorney in Tempe, Arizona, who has devoted his life to living by the example of Abraham Lincoln and sharing his love of Abraham with the community, including civic clubs, the Tempe Historical Society, and Arizona State's Leadership/Scholarship students.

Virtually everyone accepts that Abraham Lincoln is America's greatest president, the sixteenth president of the United States of America. Many at least know of his greatest speech, the Gettysburg Address, delivered on November 19, 1863, in which he reminded us that our nation was founded on the principle that all men are created equal and that we are a government of the people, by the people, for the people.

One of Glynn's passions in life is portraying Abraham Lincoln and using the president's life and words to inspire people, especially college students and children of all ages to make a difference in our world. He reminds them they are all capable of that goal and, if they doubt themselves, to look at what Abraham did with no education, no money, and no family heritage which could predict his greatness. He held an inner vision of himself that he followed.

Everyone—college students, children, and, yes, adults too—can follow the example of his life and make their dreams a reality, just as Lincoln made his dreams a reality.

He believed, as all of us can, that "right makes might" and we can combine our dreams with passion, strength and compassion to make a world of difference.

 Civility makes a difference!

CHAPTER 4: RIGHT A WRONG

"If you're not making someone else's life better, then you're wasting your time. Your life will become better by making other lives better."

—Will Smith

The Exonerator

JAMES MCCLOSKEY

Jim McCloskey served as the founder of the first organization in the United States committed to freeing the wrongly imprisoned.

During a midlife crossroads, he met the man who would change his life. A former management consultant, McCloskey had grown disenchanted with the business world. He enrolled at Princeton Theological Seminary at the age of thirty-seven. His first assignment in 1980 was as a student chaplain at Trenton New Jersey State Prison.

McCloskey said in his memoir *When Truth Is All You Have*, "Among the inmates was Jorge de los Santos, a heroin addict who'd been convicted of murder years earlier. He swore to McCloskey he was innocent and, over time, McCloskey came to believe him. With no legal or investigative training to speak of, McCloskey threw himself into the case. Two years later, thanks to those efforts, Jorge de los Santos walked free, fully exonerated."

McCloskey had found his calling. He established Centurion Ministries, the first group in America devoted to overturning wrongful convictions. "Over the last forty years, together with his staff and a team of forensic experts, lawyers, and volunteers—through tireless investigation and unflagging dedication to justice—McCloskey has freed sixty-three innocent prisoners sentenced to life in prison or to death. These inmates collectively spent 1,330 years imprisoned for the crimes of others."

In July 2020, Doubleday published his book *When Truth Is All You Have* which recounts Centurion's gripping encounters with America's criminal justice system as well as McCloskey's personal life journey that led him to this trailblazing work.

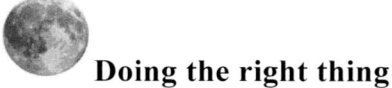 **Doing the right thing!**

James McCloskey
Founder
Centurian Ministries

A Modern-Day Tale of David Vs. Goliath

By Paula Pedene

In 2010, after sixteen years as a public affairs officer at the Phoenix VA Health Care System, Paula Pedene realized that staff morale and veteran's services were both on the decline. Senior leaders were mismanaging funds, putting their wants ahead of the needs of the veterans, and ruining the department's hard-won reputation as a high-quality health care provider.
Many of the staff noticed this and, with the help of Dr. Sam Foote, director of another local VA Health Care Clinic, they worked together to expose the mismanagement, quietly forcing the director and associate director to retire.

This should have been the end but, sadly, it was only the beginning. When new, permanent leaders came on board in 2012, they were wary of Paula and set about trying to get rid of her. She was eventually accused of a minor infraction, then demoted to a library clerk while they conducted investigations looking for a way to fire her. However, her prior stellar reputation and work ethic hindered their efforts.

Paula fought back to regain her former position. She hired legal staff that charged by the hour, and had an employee representative, Roger French, whom she also paid. Meanwhile, the VA had their own lawyers; paid staff who were at the department's beck and call. While still trying to fire her, they allowed things to drag on, making her life miserable and hoping she would quit. But by this time, with only two years to go for a full retirement, Paula wasn't about to give up.

During her banishment to the library, Paula began to hear stories of excessive waits and delays for veterans to receive help. Dr. Foote had also been hearing stories and was verifying his own information. Once again, the two of them joined forces to expose what they had learned: the "fourteen-day access to care for Veterans" was nowhere near true. In fact, for many new patients, the waits for appointments were often between six months to more than a year. What's worse, up to forty patients may have died while waiting for VA care in Phoenix.

After reporting their findings to various relevant government agencies with no results, Dr. Foote decided the only way to get the story out was for him to retire and expose it. Paula's employee representative and others joined the cause and the media took it from there. The VA Wait Time Scandal soon hit the national news. An ongoing investigation revealed that 110 of the 156 VA hospitals nationwide were involved in the scandal.

Paula eventually won her case against "whistleblower reprisal" and received a settlement in 2014.

 All veterans thank you!

A Man, A City, A Cemetery

JERRY BROCK

By Kara Bland

Jerry Brock: businessman, resident of the city of Tempe, Arizona, and advocate of Double Butte Cemetery in his city. No, he's not dead. He has lived in Tempe almost all of his life. "When I die, I want to be buried here," he said.

Jerry was nine when his family moved to Tempe in 1949. He attended Tempe Grammar School but left school after eighth grade and worked in his dad's salvage yard. The rest is history. Jerry went on to start his own auto salvage business, sold it, and opened an auto parts business, Brock Supply. He built it from a one-man operation into an international distributor. At eighty-one, he still works there.

Double Butte Cemetery is where many of the city's pioneer and civil leaders are buried, including former governor John Howard Pyle, who once called the cemetery "Tempe's Arlington."

So much of the city's history is here, governors, city leaders, doctors, firefighters, police officers, teachers, and veterans. People from various ethnic groups were buried alongside one another at a time when it didn't happen, generations of Arrendondos, Aribgus, and Valenzuelas, as well as Native Americans and Japanese Americans, evidence of how they worked and lived together in the city's early days.

Jerry has donated to the Tempe Historic Preservation Foundation to help preserve this historic landmark and other city projects for years. His giving back started when he was a young businessman. He would read a newspaper story about a child hit by a car, clip out the article, and send it with one hundred dollars to the family.

He has always tried to do things for other people. Jerry said, "I'm not going to leave this Earth without leaving some of that money to other people."

Jerry Brock—a man who never forgot where he came from!

"Jerry Brock, Tempe, Arizona"
The Arizona Republic, July 16, 2020
Karina.Bland@arizonarepublic.com

Chapter 5: Giving Life

"Never underestimate the difference *you* can make in the lives of others. Step forward, reach out, and help. This week, reach to someone that might need a lift."

—Pablo

Get in the Game

ANDY TALLEY BONE MARROW FOUNDATION

By Andy Dzurinko

In 1992, Head Coach Andy Talley was heading to the Villanova Football office at five thirty in the morning. While driving, he listened to WIP talk radio in Philadelphia, Pennsylvania, hosting an oncologist as the guest. The doctor was talking about the need for bone marrow donors. This sparked the coach's interest and his ongoing commitment to register donors.

The coach had ninety healthy players on his team he felt could be donors, so he called the doctor in New Jersey, asked about doing a bone marrow drive at Villanova. So it all started. Coach Talley contacted coaches in the area and asked if they would get involved. They said yes. Then Temple Hospital reached out and formed a partnership with him.

Since 2008, the coach's Get In the Game, Save a Life (GITG) program and the Andy Talley Bone Marrow Foundation (2010) have registered 104,000 donors. Exactly 534 GITG registrants have been identified as a patient's "perfect match" and also donated their stem cells or marrow. These young men followed through with their commitment and gave someone a second chance at life.

Thanks to the power of college football and support of hundreds of coaches and players nationwide, GITG has grown to become one of the best recruiters of stem cell/marrow donors in the world.

You, too, can get excited about what you heard or read that can make a difference in the lives of others!

www.talleybonemarrow.org

Andy Dzurinko

A Journey of Inspiration in Tackling Cancer

BRADIE JAMES

Dallas Cowboys linebacker Bradie James isn't making a flashy fashion statement when he hits the field every October in pink cleats, gloves, and wristbands. Rather, he's memorializing his mother, Etta James, who died of breast cancer in 2001 when Bradie was playing football for Louisiana State University.

"My mom's cancer was detected too late, and we didn't know what treatment options were available," James says. In 2007, he created Bradie James' Foundation 56, his player number, to "help families [avoid] going through what my family went through."

Since then, the Dallas-based foundation has raised about $500,000 from an annual gymnastics meet at LSU, a casino night in Dallas, and personal donations. Intended to provide education, therapy, and other services for breast cancer patients, survivors, and their families, grants have been made to Louisiana and Texas breast cancer facilities like the Methodist Dallas Medical Center. The facility used its $71,000 grant to fund yoga and art-therapy classes, a resource center for early detection and treatment options, and a mobile mammography van that has screened 4,000 women a year in the Dallas and Fort Worth communities. At James' request, Methodist is also developing a men's support group, which will begin in the fall.

"Bradie doesn't just want to give money," says Allison Vo, cancer program manager at Methodist. "He wants to make the patients' and the families' experiences better."

During football season, James, a nine-year pro, says his mother is never far from his mind. "I carry my mother's strength on and off the field," he says. "Breast cancer doesn't have an off-season."

 Another difference maker!

Bradie James
Liferich Publishing
www.liferichpublishing.com

Andy Dzurinko

A Call to Action

KIRK BAXTER, HIV/AIDS PIONEER

By Glen Spencer

Kirk Baxter should not be alive today. When he was a college student at Arizona State University (1978–1982) and leading efforts to establish school-sanctioned LGBTQ student organizations on campus, he learned of his HIV diagnosis. Understandably, Kirk began to contemplate his mortality and how to respond to this news at a time when his prognosis was death in fewer than three years.

Not to be deterred, Kirk devoted his energies to AIDS activism in Arizona and in Washington D.C., calling upon our government to respond to the AIDS crisis. He went on to form Phoenix Body Positive to provide life-saving wellness services to people living with HIV. At the time, medication to treat the condition was limited to AZT, which we now know was more toxic than helpful. Under Kirk's tireless leadership Phoenix Body Positive grew into a research institution conducting clinical trials for HIV therapies, and a hallmark of the HIV service community in Phoenix. Kirk continued to act as its executive director until 2005. Today the same organization operates as Southwest Center for HIV/AIDS, and continues a tradition of service with an array of HIV preventions and treatments. These programs serve more than 15,000 people annually.

Kirk Baxter has led countless community efforts in Phoenix's LGBTQ and HIV communities, including helping to return AIDS Walk Arizona to our community and founding Equality Arizona. He remains active in HIV services as a board member of HEAL International and as a member of the City of Phoenix

Fast Track Cities Ad Hoc Committee. Over the course of Kirk's forty-year career and activities in Phoenix, he has been and continues to be the most recognized and foremost advocate for HIV programming and LGBTQ rights in Arizona.

While some people recede from the world due to life-threatening challenges, only a handful accept the call to action to do more. Kirk's accomplishments in Phoenix are only surpassed by his kindness, humility, and commitment to make a difference in people's lives.

 **The LGBTQ community thanks you!**

Glen Spencer, Executive Director
Aunt Rita's Foundation
1101 N. Central Ave., #212
Phoenix, AZ 85004

Andy Dzurinko

The Power of Compassion

MAURICE STOKES/JACK TWYMAN

By Mike Vaccaro

Maurice Stokes was the NBA's Rookie of the Year in 1956 for the Rochester Royals. He became an All-Star when he moved to Cincinnati, and he averaged 16.4 points and 17.3 rebounds. At age twenty-four, Stokes was well on his way to becoming one of the greatest players in the league's history.

But on March 12, 1958, Stokes fell and banged his head during the Royals regular season finale. A few days later, on a small plane ride home from Detroit for a playoff game, he took ill. By the time he reached the hospital he was fully paralyzed, diagnosed with post traumatic encephalopathy. On April 6, 1970, he suffered a heart attack and died two months shy of his thirty-seventh birthday.

Stokes is one of the heartbreaking stories in the history of American sports, but one of the most redeeming, too, thanks to Stokes' friendship with Jack Twyman, a fellow All Star on the Royals. The two men weren't especially close, but Stokes' accident changed that.

Twyman lived year-round in Cincinnati while the Stokes family was in Pittsburgh. Soon after the diagnosis, Twyman agreed to become Stokes' legal guardian. What followed was one of the most extraordinary friendships ever formed.

One day Jack was asked why he'd decided to make such a remarkable commitment to Maurice. He shrugged his shoulder and said, "Maurice needed someone, I became that someone."

That phrase "became that someone," all these years later, has become the motto of Saint Francis University in Loretta, Pennsylvania.

Although Saint Francis had to postpone its celebration of Stokes' life in 2020, it's a message never more relevant than in these turbulent uncertain days. The pandemic has served as a call for each person to become their best self. Father Van Tassel, the Saint Francis president, says we can become that.

You, too, can become your best self!

Mike Vaccaro, mvaccaro@nypost.com, April 5, 2020

Maurice Stokes, Westinghouse High School, Pittsburgh, Pennsylvania

Jack Twyman, Central Catholic High School, Pittsburgh, Pennsylvania

Andy Dzurinko

COVID-19 Drives Aid to Arizona Indian Reservations

STEPHEN LOUIS

By Richard Obert

Gilbert Higley Arizona high school football defensive end Stephen Louis couldn't watch the news coming out of Northern Arizona and not do something.

His mother is Navajo and stepfather Hopi. He knew there were limited resources on the reservations, that many live without running water and electricity, and some people have long drives to the nearest grocery store.

With the spread of COVID-19 making the Navajo Nation one of the biggest hotspots in the country—enough to warrant weekend curfews under quarantine—Louis, in early June 2020, started a donation drive to provide relief to people on the reservations.

"I was blown away when donations started rolling in, not just from the Higley community, but from places like Texas, Vermont, Missouri, and California," Louis said.

Through June 20, 2020, Louis had collected roughly 5,000 pounds of food, water, pet food, cleaning supplies, diapers, and baby food. The efforts collected $52,000 in monetary donations, all divided among the Hopi, Navajo, and Hualapai reservations in Northern Arizona.

Parents delivered products to the Hopi reservation on June 24, while out-of-state people donated online via Amazon.

"It's a good feeling knowing we made a positive impact on the lives of the people from my tribe and nearby tribes," Louis said.

How driven are you to help others in your community?

RichardObert@ArizonaRepublic.com
Article 7/2/2020
The Arizona Republic

Andy Dzurinko

Difference Makers in World War II

NAVAJO CODE TALKERS

By Mack Dean

Communication is one of the most important components in any war. No matter what troop size, or the distance from other troops, everyone must know when they need to attack and when to withdraw. If the enemy knows what you're planning, where you are, and what you're doing, you will not only lose the element of surprise, but the enemy can attack and destroy you.

From the need to incorporate more advanced encryption into field operations in World War II came the *Navajo Code Talkers* program. During World War II, encryption or code was extremely important for communication. The problem at the time was that, even when codes were used, they were often broken by the enemy. In 1942, Philip Johnston came up with a code based on the Navajo language he thought was unbreakable. Johnston, the son of a Protestant missionary, spent much of his childhood on a Navajo reservation, learning the language and customs of the people. In adulthood, he became an engineer working for the city of Los Angeles, but also gave lectures about the Navajo people.

One day while reading the newspaper, he saw a story about people trying to come up with a way to code military communications. This story gave Johnson an idea. The next day, he went to Camp Elliot where he presented his code idea to the area signal officer Lt. Col. James E. Jones.

Skeptical, Jones pointed out previous attempts to create codes using Native American languages. The problem was their languages didn't include military terms. The officer worried about using English terms in conjunction with the Navajo language because, if he were to code everything in Navajo but used the term "machine gun" the enemy could still decipher the code.

Johnson had another idea, he figured that instead of just adding the term machine gun along with the Navajo language, one could add "rapid fire gun," or something that could be easily constructed using Navajo language. Jones recommended this be demonstrated to Major General Clayton B. Vogel and it was successful. A "pilot project" with thirty Navajos began to test out the code.

The recruiters for the program visited the Navajo reservation and selected thirty for the project. Many of the Navajo Code Talkers had never been outside the reservation, which made the move more difficult.

After the code was created, they tested it over and over again. It was essential for the code to be perfect because one mistranslated word could lead to thousands of deaths. After the first twenty-nine Navajo Code Talkers mastered the code, they were sent to Guadalcanal to use the new code in combat while one of them remained behind to train the future code talkers.

Johnson couldn't participate in the creation of the code because he was a civilian but he soon offered to enlist if he would be allowed to work on the program. He was accepted and took over the training part of the program.

Andy Dzurinko

The project was a success and permission was soon given to recruit unlimited members into the Navajo Code Talkers program. A total of 50,000 people lived in the Navajo Nation and, by the end of World War II, 420 Navajo men served as code talkers.

 America thanks you!

"Thank You, Navajo Code Talkers," *People* magazine,
Mack Dean, March 27, 2019,
www.worldwar2facts.org/navajo-code-talkers.html

Monument to Navajo Code Talkers
Window Rock, Arizona

Aiding Puerto Rico/ Latin American Countries

ROBERTO CLEMENTE, #21 PITTSBURGH PIRATES

Roberto Clemente grew up in Puerto Rico as the son of a sugar farmer. He appeared in fifteen baseball All-Star games, and he became the first Latin American player to reach 3,000 hits.

But Clemente's humanitarian work off the field shone just as brightly as his athletic ability. During off-seasons, he organized and donated to charities to bring aid to Puerto Rico and other Latin American countries. He often delivered baseball equipment and food to those in need. He also made access to sports fields available at no cost to Puerto Rican youth. Helping children, those living in poverty, was important to him.

Clemente said, "Any time you have an opportunity to make a difference in this world and you don't, you are wasting your time on this Earth."

On December 31, 1972, doing what he loved to do, helping others, he tragically died in a plane crash while en route to deliver aid to earthquake victims in Nicaragua. He was thirty-eight years old. The Pittsburgh Pirates started an annual "Day of Giving" in his honor.

 Missed but not forgotten!

www.globalarizona.org
November 21, 2019

Chapter 6:
30 Sister Cities Honorees

"In Africa there is a concept known as 'ubuntu,' the profound sense that we are human only through the humanity of others, that if we are to accomplish anything in this world it will in equal measure be due to the work and achievements of others."

—Nelson Mandela, South African anti-apartheid revolutionary, political leader and philanthropist

JOHN ENRIGHT—KAFAKUMBA TRAINING CENTER

John is the son of missionary parents and has served as a missionary in Africa since 1977. He is a licensed pilot and coordinates the Wings of the Morning aviation program, which involves funding, flying, and giving support to the people of Zambia. Together with his wife, Kendra, he founded the Kafakumba Training Center with a focus on organic farming.

In 2005, with help from others, they purchased seven acres of immature banana trees on the outskirts of Ndola, Zambia, where they live. The banana farm is very successful as is the fish hatchery and the manufacturing operation of high-end woodworking products they have introduced. Through teaching joint-ownership and profit-sharing concepts they are helping fuel a sustainable income and productive life for these people.

John Enright is planting more than trees, he is planting seeds of hope.

DR. JAMES JACKSON—PROJECT C.U.R.E.

Dr. Jackson journeyed to Brazil as an economic consultant for the U.S. government in 1987. While there, he observed long lines of sick people waiting to enter a small clinic. Once inside, he learned that children, parents, and grandparents were being turned away for lack of even the most basic medical supplies. When he returned home, he collected 250,000 dollars' worth of donated surplus medical supplies in his garage and delivered a forty-foot, ocean-going container to Brazil at his own expense.

He then founded Project C.U.R.E. Today his organization has expanded its collection points throughout America and is the world's largest distributer of donated medical supplies and equipment to developing nations around the globe. Project

C.U.R.E. volunteers and staff are Ambassadors of Hope to millions of people and are currently sending supplies to Timbuktu, Mali, Tempe's sister city.

MONA PURDY—SHARE YOUR SOLES

Mona founded Share Your Soles, a charitable foundation that distributes clean and gently used shoes to impoverished people throughout the world. In 1999, she traveled through Central America and saw children painting tar on the soles of their bare feet so they could run a race during their village festival. She happened to meet an American orthopedic surgeon who was visiting the village. He told her if these children had shoes there would be a lot less need for him to travel to the region to perform amputations of children's infected limbs.

Upon her return home, Mona collected and used children's shoes from neighborhood schools, families, and friends and, at Christmas time, delivered them to an orphanage in Honduras. Mona's life was forever changed when one of the orphanage workers asked, "When are you coming back?"

Today, thousands of volunteers clean and prepare the shoes; and airlines, corporations, and embassies help with their transport. Mona's shoes are helping people in need all over the world.

FRANK SHANKWITZ OF MAKE-A-WISH FOUNDATION

In 1980, Frank and his coworkers at the Arizona Department of Safety helped a dying seven-year-old realize his dream of being a policeman by arranging rides in a patrol car and DPS helicopter, and presenting the boy with a custom highway patrolman's uniform. After the boy died, Frank and four others started the Make-a-Wish Foundation to grant the wishes of terminally ill children. In Arizona, the foundation has granted wishes to more than 3,000 children since 1980, and almost 200,000 kids have been served worldwide.

C. MEAD WELLES—A LEG TO STAND ON

C. Mead Welles was traveling in Indonesia when he saw three underfed and exhausted boys. Two were pulling the third boy on a garbage can lid. That boy's leg was deformed, raw and bleeding. This sad incident propelled Mead to found "A Leg to Stand On" which provides free prosthetic limbs, orthopedic devices, mobility aids, surgery, and care to children in the developing world who have lost limbs or suffer from congenital disabilities.

Since 2002, ALTSO has transformed the lives of more than 12,000 children in Africa, Asia, the Middle East, and South America.

SISTER MARILYN LACEY

Sister Lacey joined the Sisters of Mercy in 1966, and for more than twenty-five years she has worked with refugees in the United States, Africa, and Southeast Asia. She has dedicated her life to making the world a more welcoming place for persons forced to leave their homelands because of war or persecution. One of her projects was the resettlement of the Lost Boys of Sudan.

In 2008, she founded Mercy Beyond Borders to transform the lives of women and children in South Sudan because "it was by far the most devastated place I'd ever seen in my decades of doing refuge work." In 2012, MBB expanded into Haiti to help the thousands displaced by the earthquake.

MBB provides education, microenterprise, improved child and maternal health programs, and scholarships.

Andy Dzurinko

Charlotte Gould

This daring young teen was born with a cleft lip and palate and has undergone multiple surgeries to correct it. When she was seven her grandmother gave her a sewing machine, and Charlotte began creating "companion dolls" for children facing surgery and other medical challenges. She knew surgery was scary and something soft to snuggle with would be of great comfort. She has now created hundreds of dolls. Charlotte is also a philanthropist, as she donates proceeds from her doll sales to various cleft charities.

Hans Vielberth—Hans Vielberth Foundation

Hans grew up in war-torn Germany and has always been a friend of America. He embraced the Sister City programs with Tempe and with other cities around the world. As a successful businessman he could have lived in opulence.

He chose instead to share his success. He has donated millions to the University of Regensburg for scholarships. He led a book drive for Odessa, Ukraine when he learned all of the city's books had been destroyed by Communists. More than 1,000,000 books were collected and trucked to Odessa at his expense.

Irma Turtle—Turtlewill Foundation

Irma was a successful advertising executive who began to offer specialized tours to remote areas of the world, especially in Africa. As she began to see the great need for healthcare, education, and basic needs such as animals to replenish family herds after drought, she went to work.

She asked herself, *Who will help these people?* The answer: Turtlewill, the foundation she started.

Irma has raised millions of dollars to build schools, hospitals, medical clinics and continues to make a world of difference.

AUSTIN GUTWEIN—HOOPS OF HOPE

Austin was only nine years old when he learned that more than 2,000 children were orphaned every school day by the HIV/AIDS virus. He wanted to help, so he started a basketball shoot-a-thon in his neighborhood. He shot 2,057 baskets, and quickly raised approximately $3,000. He partnered with World Vision, an international relief organization, and founded Hoops of Hope.

Today, Hoops of Hope has raised millions of dollars, and continues to build schools, hospitals, and clinics to help the sick and impoverished people of Zambia, Africa. Sometimes one person can make a difference, and sometimes that one person is a child.

CINDY MCCAIN—HALO TRUST, OPERATION SMILE

Cindy is a life-long humanitarian. In the 1990s, she founded the American Voluntary Medical Team that organized missions to disaster-struck or war-torn third-world countries. They completed fifty-five missions.

In 1991, the AVMT went to Bangladesh to provide assistance after a cyclone. It was here Cindy found a baby girl who would have died without medical treatment. She brought the baby and another child in desperate need back to Arizona and the McCains adopted the baby. Bridget is now a happy and healthy young woman.

Cindy also sits on the board of Operation Smile, an organization that mobilizes volunteers worldwide to repair childhood facial deformities. She has participated in medical missions to Morocco, Vietnam, and India, and serves on the board of directors for HALO Trust which works to remove land mines in war-torn areas.

BARBARA AND DON LIEM—FRIENDS OF THE ORPHANS

Tempe, Arizona, residents Barbara and Don Leim are well known for their passion for volunteer activities, especially their devotion to Friends of the Orphans, a fundraising organization dedicated to improving the lives of orphaned, abandoned, and disadvantaged children through Nuestros Pequeños Hermanos, Spanish for "Our Little Brothers and Sisters." This organization houses impoverished children throughout Latin America, the Caribbean, and South America, providing stable group homes where they receive education and a loving support system.

Barbara and Don first became involved in 1973 when they traveled to a Friends of the Orphans home near Cuernavaca. Through the years, they have raised millions of dollars to benefit Friends of the Orphans. Former pequeños volunteers include educators, doctors, accountants, carpenters, farmers, mechanics, artists, administrators, and social workers. All of the homes strive to be self-sufficient, and most operate their own schools, clinics, gardens, and farms. Whatever the homes are unable to provide comes from donations from caring friends worldwide, like Barbara and Don Liem.

CHRISTA BRELSFORD —CHRISTA'S ANGELS

Christa, an ASU graduate and doctoral student at Arizona State University School of Sustainability, worked in Haiti with a literacy program when the Port-au-Prince earthquake struck in January 2010. More than three million people were affected: 230,000 died and more than a million left homeless.

At the time the earthquake hit, Christa and her brother Julian were volunteering with Heads Together Haiti in Darbonne, just south of Port-au-Prince. Julian and others escaped, but Christa fell and concrete slabs collapsed, trapping her legs. Julian and two Haitians worked some ninety minutes to free her. Once they pulled Christa from the rubble, she needed medical assistance. One of their friends owned a motorbike, and they transported her two miles to a U.N. peacekeeping mission. As one friend drove the bike, another sat on the back holding Christa. She was then airlifted to Florida where she underwent four surgeries and her right foot was amputated. Christa is grateful to be alive and became even more determined to help the people of Haiti. Upon her return to Tempe, Arizona, she formed a foundation called Christa's Angels to help Haitians recover from the earthquake, to rebuild the school operated by Haiti Partners, and to provide opportunities for the Haitians who rescued her.

The school is being rebuilt and funds are now needed to pay each of the seventeen teachers eighty dollars per month, and to pay for the students' and teachers' daily lunch—fifty-two cents per person—often their only meal of the day.

GUY DAVIDSON—GRACE COMMUNITY CHURCH/INTERNATIONAL MISSIONS

This popular pastor served the Tempe, Arizona, community for decades, helped found two of its largest churches, and was instrumental in many international missions as well. Pastor Davidson traveled the world assisting in establishing hospitals, schools, clinics, and orphanages. He served on the boards of Food for the Hungry, Samaritan's Purse, World Medical Mission, and others. He was been instrumental in recruiting and sending short-term volunteer medical teams to many third world nations, areas of natural disasters, and war-torn areas of civil unrest.

While at Grace Community Church in Tempe, he inspired the congregation to participate in various projects, including the sponsorship of a one-year program building more than one hundred church community centers in India that would include schools, clean water, and health education programs.

In addition, Guy Davidson was instrumental in establishing and supporting hospitals and/or clinics in the Ivory Coast, Lebanon, Jordan, Angola, Ethiopia, Kenya, and Taiwan. He helped establish orphanages in Ertrea, El Salvador, Egypt, Taiwan, Mexico, and India. He has raised funds for buildings and student scholarships for three schools in Calcutta, India. These serve more than 2,000 students of families in the inner city, the poorest of the poor.

Into his eighties, he remained committed to training and development to help the people of Cuba.

LISA HOPPER—WORLD CARE

The story began when Lisa managed the radiology department of George Washington University Hospital in Washington D.C., and conducted medical assessments around the world. She saw the need for basic medical aid; food, shelter, and education. She realized that, without proper access to education, people would never be able to rise out of poverty. As she traveled, she brought with her supplies for children, supplies she gathered in her home.

After moving to Tucson and taking a position with the University of Arizona Medical Center, she began collecting materials in her garage. In 1996, she put all of her retirement savings into starting an organization called World Care "dedicated to providing humanitarian aid in areas of education, health, emergency relief, and environment." She has devoted herself to its development.

Since then, World Care has collected more than fifteen million pounds of resources valued at more than forty million dollars and redirected them away from landfills and into World Care programs. The organization was one of the first on the scene at Ground Zero, providing supplies and personnel.

Today, World Care has come a long way from that garage. It provides supplies to more than 150 local nonprofits and reaches more than sixty countries around the globe.

TERRY AND ANNE GUERRANT—
THE GUERRANT FOUNDATION

Terry and Anne Guerrant created the Guerrant Foundation in 2005 with the mission to create "lasting change by uplifting the poorest of the world's poor through small loans for micro enterprise." Anne was a professional tennis player who traveled the world, and was moved by the extreme poverty she saw in third-world nations. After visiting a micro credit lending program in India, Anne and her husband Terry, created the Guerrant Foundation to help women and families improve their lives through tiny loans to start a business. Their goal is to personally give a million dollars and raise another million to help this important cause. So far more than 40,000 small business have been created in countries around the world.

DERRECK KAYONGO—GLOBAL SOAP PROJECT

Derreck's Global Soap Project collects used hotel soap bars, reprocessing it to save lives in impoverished countries. Since 2009, the Atlanta-based nonprofit has provided about 150,000 bars of soap for communities in ten countries, including Haiti, Kenya, and Afghanistan. Kayongo, a Uganda native, considers the soap he provides for poverty-stricken children "a first line of defense" to help fight disease.

EDGAR RODAS—CINTERANDES MOBILE MEDICINE IN ECUADOR

As a medical student in the 1960s, Dr. Rodas was inspired by Project HOPE and other programs that brought medical aid directly to the people. When he became Minister of Health for Ecuador, he was frustrated by the lack of care for "marginalized" people. He wanted to find a way to bring free medical assistance to the poor and isolated peoples of his country. His dream was to create a health clinic on wheels to travel to the remote areas of the Andes Mountains, the tiny fishing villages, and the settlements of the Ecuadorian Amazon.

He began assembling a small medical team that traveled to small hospitals in the Amazon jungle. Ten missions and three years later, his dream of a Mobile Surgical Unit came true. The MSU team includes medical doctors who volunteer their time, as well as medical and nursing students from around the world.

Since the Cinterandes Foundation began in 1995, more than 50,000 people have been treated and more than 8,000 surgeries have been performed.

DR. RAUL OSORIO—THE OSORIO FOUNDATION

As a young man Dr. Osorio immigrated to America where he attended high school and college. After graduating from medical school he joined the U.S. Air Force serving as a flight surgeon. In the early 1980s, he began organizing medical missions to his native Peru, bringing modern medicine to impoverished areas in and around his hometown, Caraz. The missions began with a few doctors and nurses, and grew to include teams of more than sixty members. Over the years, Dr. Osorio led dozens of people, young and old, to provide medical care and supplies to the poor areas of Peru.

DR. BRIAN AND KERI DEGUZMAN—4MATI FOUNDATION

When the deGuzmans traveled to Addis Ababa, Ethiopia, to adopt their four children, they saw children begging on the streets and families living in deplorable conditions. They knew they had to help. When they returned home, they created the 4Mati Foundation, which supports and develops programs targeting education, health care, and orphan support for many of the six million orphaned children in Ethiopia. They are working to create self-sustaining projects and teach communities how to care for their own people. A food production facility has been completed and a school which will serve some 2,000 children.

DR. JOHN GILLAN

Dr. John Gillan has conducted and personally financed more than twenty-five dental missions abroad, helping the forgotten and under-served. He brings his own supplies, including books, to share with professors and local dentists. He goes where he is most needed and treats patients "in the bush."

Dr. Gillan has traveled to Romania, Kosovo and Cameroon. His wife Cindy and his children have accompanied him on most of these missions.

MARIA KELLER—READ INDEED

When Maria was eight years old she learned that some children in the world did not have any books of their own. She couldn't imagine such a thing, and vowed to collect and distribute one million books by the time she was eighteen. She surpassed that goal by the time she fourteen.

She founded Read Indeed and has distributed books to children in America and several other countries around the world.

RAVEEN ARORA

Raveen Arora has been honored many times for his humanitarian work donating time, money, skills, and compassion to people trapped in poverty—those without education, medical services, and without hope. A native of India, Raveen has aided people in Nepal, Bhutan, Bangladesh, and other countries. When he settled in Arizona in 2002, he even began distributing bottles of water to the homeless on hot summer days.

MALLORY BROWN—WORLD CLOTHES LINE, AND TRAVEL MAL

This social entrepreneur, adventure traveler, and global humanitarian has conducted charity campaigns in twenty-two countries. Mallory began her career at age twenty-four by founding World Clothes Line to bring a piece of new clothing to children around the world who had never had anything new.

She extended her reach to found Travel Mal. For her 30th birthday she went to Ethiopia to raise thirty thousand dollars to help thirty women start their own businesses. She actually raised forty-one thousand dollars in twenty-four hours

Her goal is to connect charitable givers to incredible causes around the world and to inspire the next generation of givers.

DENNIS GERLACH—FLYING SAMARITANS

Dennis Gerlach is an electrical engineer by profession. He is also a pilot and a dedicated humanitarian. Since 2012, he has served as president of the Flying Samaritans, Phoenix Chapter—a volunteer, health-oriented organization that works with local professionals to provide medical and dental care for the impoverished people living in remote areas of Baja in Mexico.

The organization's 150 volunteers are physicians, dentists, dental hygienists, physician assistants, nurse practitioners, nurses, pharmacists, and other healthcare professionals and volunteers. These "Sams" provide basic medical and dental services, along with medications from their pharmacies, all at no charge to their patients. Plus, they pay their own expenses. Donated funds are applied to equipment, medicines, and supplies for the ten clinics provided each year. Dennis has flown more than sixty missions to Baja and logged some 450 hours as a Sam.

INES AND TRACEY ALLEN—IMAHELPS

While growing up in Equador, Ines lost her brother to illness because the family could not afford medical care. Once in the United States, and after having volunteered with the Flying Samaritans, Ines and her husband decided to found IMAHelps, an organization that would provide similar missions in Central and South America.

Andy Dzurinko

MARK HUERTA

Mark leads a team of Arizona State University students and faculty who responded to a call from a school in Bangladesh where the water was believed to be contaminated by arsenic. Mark and his team soon determined arsenic was not the problem. To help, they provided the school with readily available technology. The team moved on to develop new water filters for villages in Dominican Republic and a small village near Cusco, Peru.

Mark said, "To see those kids drink clean water for the first time is the most rewarding feeling you can ever have."

KENTON LEE

Kenton observed a little girl in Kenya trying to walk in shoes that were much too small for her. She had cut the front of the shoes off and her toes hung out. He learned that shoes were precious—needed to protect feet from parasites, injury and disease, and in many cases were a requirement to attend school. Some 300 million children in the world do not have shoes, and those who do quickly outgrow them.

Kenyon thought about a shoe that would grow as the child grew, but was unable to generate an interest with shoe manufacturers. He then assembled his own team and, after five years of trying, produced a prototype that would work. Thus, he founded Because International. To-date, more than 250,000 pairs of the "shoe that grows" have been distributed in one hundred countries.

KATHI JUNTUNEN

Upon seeing photos of starving and abandoned children in the streets of Haiti, Kathi traveled there in 2005, determined to do something to help. The next year, she founded Chances4Children, lived in Haiti for a year, and has since made some eighty trips there. It was during one of these trips she and her husband met three children they later adopted.

Chances4Children now serves more than 5,000 children. Programs work through local church communities to provide food and clean water, medical clinics, orphan care, education, and empowerment programs for women.

MICHAEL AND MICHELLE TESSENDORF—
ORCHARD: AFRICA

While living in Mifikeng, South Africa, the Tessendorfs found children rummaging for food in the city garbage dump. Their church began cooking food to feed about thirty children. That soon grew, and Orchard: Africa was born.

The program worked through local churches by training pastors and staff to develop gardening and agricultural programs to grow food; and provide compassionate care for orphans, the sick, and the elderly.

Now, a ministry in its own right, Orchard: Africa extends its reach to more than 600 community churches and one hundred funded programs in sub-Saharan Africa. It provides hope and change for thousands of families.

Andy Dzurinko

Epilogue

By Anne Montgomery

COVID-19 has changed our world and while most of us will immediately consider the hardships caused by the virus, perhaps there are some silver linings that will result from the pandemic.

It's easy to see that our everyday health might improve, if only for the spotlight on hygiene practices. Even the youngest among us now understands the importance of diligent hand washing and the necessity of social distancing to prevent the spread of germs. Maybe, in our new-normal world, people will be healthier for that fact alone.

Another positive is volunteering. While close to twenty-five percent of people say they volunteer, it seems, anecdotally at least, more of us are giving our time to others. Perhaps, many of us, freed from the constraints imposed by our daily routines, are simply finding more time to do good. Or maybe the act of helping our neighbors boosts our own feelings of well-being. Whatever the reason, there seem to be more people out giving others a life, as we weather this new world.

COVID-19 and the Black Lives Matter protests have shaken us from our complacency. As a former high school teacher of twenty years, I can tell you the majority of my students looked no further than next Friday night's football game, or were content spending hours engrossed in video games. Now, young people have been forced to sit up and take notice of what's happening in the world around them and many, for the first time, are participating in movements bigger than themselves. As a teacher who often spoke about the importance of our First

Amendment rights, I can say prior to the demonstrations, these young people didn't seem to grasp the importance of "the right of the people to peaceably assemble." They do now.

Our country, and many others around the world, are currently faced with twin enemies. One, an invisible invader who sickens our bodies. Two, a marauder who poisons our souls. These adversaries—illness and bigotry—can bring us down. But they don't have to. Around the world, people are joining hands and voices, shouting out against intolerance and racism. It seems the narrow-minded among us are losing the battle. At least, I hope they are.

Which brings me to the Tempe Sister Cities mission, a program that strives for better communication and understanding across the globe. We are now united in our fight against COVID-19, a foe that has no respect for national boundaries. Extinguishing racism, as well, is a battle being waged worldwide. The Tempe Sister cities initiative has "been making peace through understanding... one friendship at a time" for almost fifty years.

"Tempe Sister Cities has been a leader of student, educational, and cultural exchanges making the goal of peace through understanding a reality." The hope is for people of all nationalities and cultures to come together and share their experiences to foster global peace. This idea is more important today than ever before.

As a former history teacher, it is my hope that years from now, when the story of this time is written, it will recall how we all united in a time of fear, frustration, and sadness, and that together we changed things for the better. And, from that future perch, we'll be able to look back and confidently say we stood up and made a difference when the people of the world needed it most.

Anne Butler Montgomery has worked as a print reporter, a teacher, an amateur sports official, and a TV sportscaster, including a stint at ESPN where she anchored "SportsCenter." Her novels include *Wild Horses on the Salt*, *The Scent of Rain*, and *A Light in the Desert*. Montgomery is a foster mom to three sons. When she can, she indulges in her passions: rock collecting, scuba diving, and playing her guitar.

 **A trailblazer!**

Inspiration

"You Gotta Believe"

A VIGNETTE FROM ANDY'S BOOK
THE POWER OF OPTIMISM

Andy Dzurinko, CLU, MEd, with August Aquila, Ph.D.

Stay positive and active!

In his best-selling book *Anatomy of an Illness*, Norman Cousins described his remarkable recovery from a life-threatening disease. He explained the effective use of positive emotions—hope, love, laughter, faith, and a robust will to live—to combat a serious illness with recovery odds of one in five hundred. The medical establishment at that time was just beginning to realize the power of what people believe could radically affect their state of being.

In *The Power of Positive Thinking*, Norman Vincent Peale observed, "if you think the best, you can attain it." He believed thoughts are powerfully linked to one's self-image. He claimed the picture a person habitually carries in his or her mind can result in the person becoming that image.

While in Indianapolis, I had the privilege of meeting Wilma Rudolph as we lived in the same neighborhood. The dramatic story about the three-time Olympic gold medal winner exemplifies the remarkable power of our thoughts and beliefs. Wilma was the twentieth of twenty-two children in her family. From a very early age, she was taught to believe she could achieve anything if she really wanted it. Since her family was very poor, she had little more than her dreams in which to believe. At age four, she contracted double pneumonia and scarlet fever resulting in paralysis of her left leg. Doctors held little hope she would ever walk without the aid of a leg brace. But Wilma was determined to walk and run like other children.

At age nine, she was able to remove the leg brace, and by age thirteen, she could walk unaided. She entered foot races regularly, but always finished last. Everyone told her to quit racing. But Wilma wouldn't relinquish her dream to win. Eventually, she won a race, and she continued to win one after another until the girl who was told she would never walk won three Olympic gold medals.

No matter what you do, you have to believe in yourself. If you don't, how can you expect others to believe in you? Try telling yourself one positive thing each day. It can be as nonspecific as "something good is going to happen today." Make sure it is a positive thought. If you don't send yourself these positive messages, what messages are you sending? What is the picture you habitually carry in your mind? There is no greater step you can take toward creating inner wealth than developing a positive self-image.

 **It works!**

"The Laughter Cure"

A VIGNETTE FROM ANDY'S BOOK
LOL—LAUGH OUT LOUD: FEEL GOOD AND LIVE LONGER

James Harris, M.D. and Andy Dzurinko, CLU, MEd

Don't ever lose your sense of humor!!

Robert Schimmel, a stand-up comedian, remembered the first time he walked into the Mayo Clinic in Scottsdale, Arizona, after being told he had cancer. It reminded him of the poster, "The Evolution of Man." Except what he was looking at was a row of balding, skinny, chalky-skinned chemotherapy patients with IV tubes in their arms. So much for evolution, he joked to himself. That was the beginning of the road to his recovery.

He had been fascinated by the power of laughter since he was a boy. His parents, who were Holocaust survivors, had terrific senses of humor and introduced him to some of the greatest comedians of the time. He grew up watching Jackie Gleason, Ernie Kovacs, Sid Ceasar, Jonathan Winters, the Three Stooges, and the Marx Brothers. As a kid, he learned if you could make people laugh, everyone liked you. And the feeling he got from making people laugh was addictive. He had no way of knowing the power of laughter would one day save his life.

Andy's younger brother John was diagnosed with stage-four liver cancer in June of 2004. He, too, had a great sense of humor, laughed, made people laugh and had a positive attitude. On Sunday, December 5, 2004, the last time Andy saw John, they watched *Return of the Pink Panther* starring Peter Sellers. They had a great time, laughed, and enjoyed each other. John told Andy that when he found out he had cancer, it felt like a train hit him. However, at no time did he or his beautiful wife Layla ever stop laughing. He said it helped to ease the pain and suffering, and gave hope to his family to stay positive.

He, too, was convinced, just like Robert Schimmel, that laughter helped him cope with his deadly disease. John didn't survive, but there was no doubt in his mind that laughter made a big difference in his final days. He died on December 9, 2004.

John's smile, laughter, and love of life touched a lot of people. It will always be a part of Andy's life.

 Cancer. It's no joke.

> Robert Schimmel died of injuries sustained in an auto accident on September 3, 2010. His cancer was in remission.
>
> Robert Schimmel, *Reader's Digest*
> March 2005, pp. 128–131

"Make a World of Difference/ Sister Cities"

Words and music by Duane Moore

We can make a world of difference,
And it starts with you and me
Through cultural understanding,
We'll live in peace and harmony
And we'll celebrate our diversities,
And shine a light for all the world to see

Over this land, and across the sea,
I can learn from you, you can learn from me
Sister Cities, hold your banners high!
Bring the world together,
One friendship at a time

Global exchange, let's learn together,
And educate our way of life
And create friendships that last forever,
Speak the language of love and do what's right
We will sing a song of international goodwill,
In a voice for all the world to hear

Andy Dzurinko

Over this land, and across the sea.
I can learn from you, you can learn from me
Sister Cities, hold your banners high!
Bring the world together,
One friendship at a time

Over this land, and across the sea,
I can learn from you, you can learn from me
Sister Cities, hold your banners high!
Bring the world together,
One friendship at a time

Sister Cities, hold your banners high!
Bring the world together,
One friendship at a time

List of Tempe, Arizona, Sister Cities

Location	Established
Skopje, North Macedonia	1971
Regensburg, Germany	1976
Lower Hutt, New Zealand	1981
Zhenjiang, China	1989
Timbuktu, Mali	1991
Beaulieu sur Mer, France	1997
Carlow, Ireland	1998
Cuenca, Ecuador	2008
Cusco, Peru	2012
Trollhättan, Sweden	2015
Agra City, India	2016

"I believe that the more you give, the more you get. It's as simple as that."

—**Nishan Rajakaruna, '08 Bucknell University**

Andy Dzurinko

Conclusion

There are many different definitions of inspiration and many different ways that people are inspired to take action that can and will help others.

One definition that I like, from vocabulary.com, is "a sudden intuition or idea or something that arouses your desire to take action."

The question is, what will it take for you to grow excited enough about something that could make a difference not only in your life but the lives of others and in your community?
Do you have the passion, commitment, and motivation to make it happen?

This desire to take action is exactly what motivated Dick Neuheisel to expand Tempe's international horizons after he was elected to the city council in 1968. It prompted him to attend a Sister Cities International Conference in San Diego which fueled his excitement further. He then approached Harry Mitchell, a teacher in Tempe, Arizona, with the idea of forming a Sister Cities program. Harry felt it would be a great way for students and teachers to get to know and learn from people in other countries. The Mayor of Skopje was the first to get involved. The year 2021 marks the fiftieth anniversary of the first visit by a delegation from Skopje, Tempe's first sister city.

"**Bringing the world together… one friendship at a time.**"

Request for Review

If you enjoy this book,
please consider jotting a review on Andy Dzurinko's
book page at Amazon.com.
Even a couple of sentences about your experience
will be most appreciated.

Also, feel free to contact Andy at
dzurinko@gmail.com or
www.thepowerofoptimism.com.

About the Author

ANDY DZURINKO, CLU, ChFC, MEd

Andy Dzurinko grew up in the once-thriving steel town of Monessen, Pennsylvania, twenty-seven miles south of Pittsburgh. From the time he played in the local Midget Football League, sports have always played a big part in Andy's life. He was an All-State lineman for the Monessen High School football team that won a conference championship in 1960. He went on to Bucknell University where, in Andy's senior year, the Bisons won the Lambert Cup, symbolic of Eastern small college football supremacy. For his many athletic accomplishments, he was inducted into Pennsylvania's Mid Mon Valley All Sports Hall of Fame in 2009.

Commissioned a second lieutenant, he served two years of active duty with the U.S. Army, including a tour in Vietnam. Returning to civilian life, he earned a masters' degree at the University of Pittsburgh where he began a ten-year coaching career that took him to Williams College and Brown University before entering the insurance industry in 1978.

Andy was director of training and regional vice president of agencies for American United Life Insurance Company in Indianapolis before relocating to Arizona in 1988 to become a general agent and personal producer for AUL. He has qualified for the Million Dollar Round Table and the National Quality Award, and been accredited as a chartered life underwriter and chartered financial consultant by The American College.

While his playing and coaching days are behind him, Andy maintains an active workout regimen and ran in his first marathon at the age of fifty-six. His bucket list after age sixty-five included: hiking Mt. Whitney, the Half Dome in Yosemite, the Grand Canyon in the United States; and, internationally, Mt. Kilimanjaro in Africa, Machu Pichu in Peru, Mt. Blanc in France, and Walking the El Camino in Spain.

While serving as executive director of Arizona Governor's Council on Health, Physical Fitness and Sports, he received the Outstanding Council Member Award from the National Association. Always willing to give back to his community with such groups as Tempe Sister Cities, Sigma Chi Fraternity Alumni, Bucknell Alumni, and the National Football Foundation, he has headed up the Frank Kush Youth Foundation for the past twenty-nine years.